The Productivity Protocol

Make Life Easier By Following The Productivity Protocol And Eliminating Procrastination In The Process

Table of Contents

Introduction

This book contains proven steps and strategies on how to improve your level of productivity through a series of protocols.

This book lists ways to increase your level of productivity in the most practical ways possible. Additionally, it gives you a deeper sense of meaning in your life. With these tips, you can be in better control of your life and things will become easier than ever. There are suggested steps for you to reach your goals – both short- and long-term goals. The suggestions can help you avoid the temptations of procrastination.

Chapter 1 – The Productivity Protocol: An Overview

To have a clear idea on what boosts one's productivity, one should follow a certain set of protocols. First, there is a need to define what protocol is.

According to an online dictionary, a protocol is an established system or procedure that sets the proper or accepted way of completing a task and dictates the rules that govern a certain situation.

Usually, nations, companies and industries have protocols, but in this book, even individuals can set their own protocols. The main focus of this book is the establishment of the Productivity Protocol. Of course, the Productivity Protocol has the main aim of boosting one's productivity. Eventually, when you get the hang of it, you can be more productive.

Without further ado, we begin with different items you might consider including in your own productivity protocol. As you can see, we are getting to the point as early as possible, because that is what productivity is all about – getting to the point and getting it done right away.

Suggested Productivity Protocol Item #1: Find your passion and choose a job in line with it.

Choose a job you are truly passionate about, and you will not have to work a single day – this is what they always tell us. Aside from making you feel good, choosing a career you are passionate about can help improve your productivity. If you love what you do, you are more likely to have greater motivation. Productivity will not suffer because not one wants to be mediocre in his passion.

Suggested Productivity Protocol Item #2: Cut down the clutter by living like a minimalist.

Imagine living in a place where there is clutter everywhere. Clutter can greatly influence your productivity because it has a big effect on your mental state, your psychological disposition, and the way you feel about yourself. Clutter leads to the lack of organization in your workplace.

Being disorganized, especially in the workplace, can lead to distraction, and distraction is one of the main enemies of productivity. Productivity suffers when you are distracted because you tend to do things you should not do. To avoid distractions, make the setting as simple as possible. Keep only the things that are truly necessary. Throw away any items that do not have a purpose.

Suggested Productivity Protocol Item #3: Wake up early.

Rising early, by virtue of logic, allows you to do more with your day. It gives you enough time to prepare for things that might arise throughout the day. You can use this extra time to prepare a list of tasks you need to accomplish. It gives you a chance to prepare physically, and it enables you to psyche yourself properly. You can tell yourself that there is nothing you cannot do. With enough time to prepare, it is tough to go wrong when it comes to productivity.

Suggested Productivity Protocol Item #4: Use the simplest possible words in writing your to-do list or task list.

Keep your to-do list simple to keep your life simple. Using vague words can only frustrate you before you even start the task. Write your goals in the simplest manner possible. When your write your tasks, imagine how you want to get the task done. By choosing your words well, completion is within your reach. Never fall into the trap of writing your task using complicated words and sentences. Complex sentence construction might discourage you in the end.

Suggested Productivity Protocol Item #5: When faced with more than one task, prioritize.

Learn how to weigh different tasks according to importance. That way, you can pass judgment regarding which tasks are the most important and which tasks can wait. This protocol item helps organize a busy schedule filled with multiple deadlines. Prioritization can do wonders if applied properly.

Suggested Productivity Protocol Item #6: Unplug for a designated portion of the day.

It is up to you to decide how much time you wish to spend offline. By being offline, you naturally get away from the inherent distractions brought about by the social media. You will realize that unplugging from the World Wide Web is an excellent practice, especially if you want to get something done. Progress is usually substantial when you are not online because you can give your full attention to what you need to do.

Suggested Productivity Protocol Item #7: Show up earlier than what is required.

Waking up earlier just to show up an hour early for a meeting may seem daunting, but it has its benefits. For example, instead of showing up in your 8 AM office at exactly 8 AM, why not show up an hour earlier? By doing that, you can plan ahead and settle into the work day more easily. By the time the clock strikes 8 AM, you are more than ready. You will be riding on a constant momentum, helping you achieve more. Showing up early also gives you time to reflect on what your work. Is it what you really want? Are you truly passionate about it?

Suggested Productivity Protocol Item #8: Review your contract and stick to the Terms of Reference stated in it.

By sticking to the TOR or the Terms of Reference, you are 100 percent sure you are not doing anyone else's work. It pays to read and re-read your contract because it reminds you of what you should do and at the same time, warns you of what you should not be doing. By sticking to your duties and responsibilities, you will be more efficient and better valued in your field in your workplace. Aside from that, you can also avoid or say no to unnecessary work.

Suggested Productivity Protocol Item #9: Begin with the more daunting tasks first.

In your timeline, you have to make sure you begin with the most challenging projects. That way, you can to channel your energy properly and by the time you are finished, the next tasks should feel easier to manage and accomplish. By arranging your tasks in decreasing difficulty, you can look forward to the next tasks without getting too exhausted because you know the work becomes easier.

Suggested Productivity Protocol Item #10: By all means, avoid meetings.

It is impossible to completely avoid meetings, but you need to remember that little is achieved during meetings because everyone is busy talking and suggesting. After airing all the suggestions, you are on your own again. If you have the power to do so, allocate the least number of minutes possible to meetings because they create little progress. However, if you find yourself in the situation wherein you are obliged to attend a meeting, make it productive by clarifying all points of discussion and asking the most important questions whenever necessary.

Chapter 2 – Workplace Organization Protocols

As mentioned in the previous chapter, clutter is one of the enemies of productivity. If you are serious about setting productivity protocols for your life and your career, you also have to learn about workplace organization. This involves a lot of measures necessary for cutting clutter.

Note that aside from your physical, intellectual, and psychological attributes as a writer, you also have to be 100 percent in sync with the physical space in which you work. If the body serves as the soul's place of abode, the space devoted for work is considered as the temple of any kind of business. Therefore, any worker should perceive the workplace as a venue of sanctity worthy of respect and dignity.

Whenever possible, one should establish a space for work in a manner that makes you feel comfortable and, at the same time, compelled to perform your duties. The elements important for the work should be lined up in a manner to enhance the level of productivity. This will ensure that all actions lead to higher returns. Therefore, a workspace that is free from distractions and clutter guarantees higher levels of productivity because you do more with less.

Overhauling your workspace in terms of organization may not be necessary. At the very most, all you have to do is to slightly adjust the things that surround you. To improve your organization and to cut down all the clutter, here are some tips:

Workplace Organization Tip #1: If you do not need it, toss it.

Be brave enough to decide whether a certain item sitting in your workspace is necessary or not. By identifying the unnecessary, you can eliminate right away. Unnecessary items can soon become clutter, and clutter leads to distraction. It is much easier to procrastinate if your space is full of clutter, and yes, it is easier to organize things in your office if you have fewer objects lying around. What should you do with the unnecessary things? The answer is quite simple: throw them away.

Workplace Organization Tip #2: Keep the soft copy and throw the printouts.

Collecting printouts is pointless because you can scan them and keep the soft copies. For one, office systems nowadays are already gearing towards total paperless transactions because they are more environmentally-friendly. Additionally, you can also scan important documents like bills, old invoices, and documents, so you can proceed with recycling the paper. To avoid the buildup of documents, why not just scan everything? You can maximize the use of technology to reduce the clutter in the workplace. In the end, fewer distractions can improve productivity significantly.

Workplace Organization Tip #3: Sync all calendars, to-do lists, and planners.

If you are keeping offline and online versions of calendars, to-do lists, and planners, you have to do your best to synchronize them all the time to avoid conflicts and confusions. This helps you efficiently monitor projects that have to be finished, tasked that need to be accomplished, meetings that have to be attended, and clients who require progress reports, and so on. If possible, drop the offline version and maximize the gifts offered by technology. All smartphones already have calendars, to-do lists, and planners you can synchronize across different kinds of platforms.

Workplace Organization Tip #4: If documents regularly come in, sort them out at least twice daily.

When you sort out documents regularly, it should only take a few minutes. Have two designated periods within the day to do this – once in the morning and once before you head home. Always be sure that the documents are processed properly and accordingly. The different papers need to be separated and classified, so you do not have any confusion down the road. Sort out papers using a system you have established, and with time, you will figure out what system best suits your needs. When you get the hang of it, you can become much more efficient.

Workplace Organization Tip #5: Clear the virtual clutter.

It is not only the real desktop you should clear of clutter. To free your mind from worries, take time to clear the virtual clutter as well. Browse through the files you have saved and check out the downloads. Certainly, there are several items you no longer need. Take the liberty to delete what is not needed, and you can reduce your virtual clutter. If there are files you might need in the future, then try to back them up on your email or onto a separate drive. For the remaining files, try your best to label them properly.

Workplace Organization Tip #6: Put labels on everything in your workspace.

To properly orient yourself, you need to put labels on the things you have decided to keep. This way, you can save time looking for the items you need. This is one of the reasons behind tip #4. When you sort items regularly, labeling and locating items becomes easier. Labeled partitions also help you become more efficient in sorting.

Workplace Organization Tip #7: Designate zones for different tasks.

Your workspace does not have to be a mess. To avoid creating clutter, label each part of your workstation, so you are properly reminded of what you can and cannot do in any particular spot. By knowing what each zone is for, you can always be in the right zone.

Chapter 3 – Decision-Making and Time Management Protocols for Improved Productivity

Everything you do – yes, there are no exceptions – leads to a decision, and delaying decisions is only further hinders productivity. When productivity suffers, a lot of problems arise, and you might not like the consequences.

Decisiveness is an important ingredient toward better productivity. Productivity can only be considered "good" or "acceptable" only if you can maintain it. Maintaining a certain productivity level can only be achieved if you make high quality decisions. This is the reason why leaders who are capable of delivering high quality decisions are the most valued people in team or even company.

This is easier said than done, of course. However, setting up a protocol for better decision making makes it easier for you to confront the crossroads and decisions. Decisions can be simple or complex. Effects of decisions can either be short-term or long-term. This is why you have to be extra careful in making them. In this chapter, you learn how to make decisions that are precise, timely, and significant.

Decision-Making Protocol #1: Be sure to align decisions you are making to the goals related to your productivity.

Keep in mind the rationale behind the necessity of making decisions. Why are you in this situation, by the way? Why do you need to make any decision?

Constantly remind yourself of the reasons because human beings are naturally inclined to forget. Revisit your goals – both personal and organizational – and align them with your productivity aims. Evaluate them every once in a while and monitor how much you have achieved so far.

Decision-Making Protocol #2: Learn how to defend, rationalize, and explain to other people how you were able to arrive at a certain decision.

Standing by one's decision is an essential component of making a decision. Making the decision is one thing – seeing through it until the end is another. It cannot be denied that aims and goals are important, but it is also important for a decision maker to understand why he is making the decision before anything else. By knowing the rationale or, you know what the best decision should be.

Decision-Making Protocol #3: Create goals that are clear and easy to follow.

Clarity is one of the most important properties or characteristics of goals. By the way, you cannot consider a goal a good one unless it is clearly stated. Goals, as previously pointed out, are the ultimate basis of sound decisions. These decisions, in turn, tell you if you are on the right path, which is later on reflected by your overall productivity.

Decision-Making Protocol #4: Be aware and embrace the fact that a well-lived life is a life full of risks.

Face reality: you have to take risks. Experts always say, "If you do not risk anything, you are actually risking everything." By being aware of the fact that risks do exist, you can be more aware of the path you need to take. You will also be less likely to feel shocked by mistakes, faults and failures. As the one who makes the decision, it is necessary for you to look at the worst scenario. If you can deal with the worst scenario, then it only means you are also ready for the best to come. Reducing the risk level is the option to take if you think you cannot deal with the worst case.

Never be afraid to create very important decisions. You have to learn this skill because, otherwise, productivity might suffer. Of course, take your time and think about your decision. Do it with care and consider all possible scenarios.

This leads us to another important point – in order to be truly productive, a person should have skills in time management and take sufficient time in mastering them. Once mastered, you will apply the principles in everything you do. The following items are the time management protocols you might consider adding to your personal list:

Time Management Protocol #1: Do your best to set deadlines for yourself and stick to them.

Deadlines are pointless if they are not respected. Therefore, each deadline you set for yourself should be treated with sanctity. Follow it to the letter. Before setting your personal deadline, you have to consider and evaluate if they are realistic and doable. If the answer is no, then you might need to adjust the deadline before finalizing it.

Time Management Protocol #2: Have fun and from time to time, make it a point to give yourself a well-deserved reward.

Whenever you finish any task, try to give yourself a pat on the back for a job well-done. If you love sweets, treat yourself to some cake, candy, or chocolates. If you think you are deprived of sleep, after doing the task, take a long and well-deserved rest. This helps you avoid burnout. Burnout is a possible problem, so you need to avoid it at all costs.

Time Management Protocol #3: If you can, avoid multitasking.

Multitasking is for computers, and you must admit the fact that as a human being, you have your limits. A human being is said to do well if he takes on tasks one at a time. When a person takes the challenge of accomplishing multiple tasks at once, there is a great chance that some details might be forgotten. A person is more efficient if he takes on one task at a time, and yes, you feel less stress if you avoid multitasking.

Time Management Protocol #4: Downtime always happens, so you have to utilize it with all efficiency possible.

Downtime is defined as the period where you are compelled to do nothing significant. However, doing nothing significant is just a state of mind. For example, when you are riding the cab on your way home, you can check your emails via your smart phone, or if you are waiting for your appointment with the dentist, you can synchronize your calendars or fix your schedule. These seemingly useless downtimes can be put to good use, after all.

Time Management Protocol #5: Make a list of tasks that need to be done.

All people who wish to improve their productivity should keep a to-do list in order to manage their time more efficiently. When making a to-do list, one has to follow some basic principles. First, consider the deadlines, which is the factor of urgency. Next, arrange them in the order of difficulty. This, on the other hand, is the factor of difficulty. By considering these two factors, you have a better idea of how to go about your tasks. You can easily partition your time each day.

By making a list, you are able to renew your commitment to better productivity. Lists can be created on a sheet of paper, on a notepad, in your computer, or even in the pre-installed calendar in your smart phone. By having one ready, you will be better organized, can make better decisions, and of course, can save more time. Ultimately, the level of productivity will surely rise.

Time Management Protocol #6: Learn how to efficiently delegate or distribute tasks, duties, and responsibilities to people you trust.

Task delegation is not a sign of being weak; it is actually a sign of working in a smart manner. It is also an indicator that you recognize capabilities and talents of the people around you. Being surrounded by reliable and competent people is a blessing you should maximize. This way, you can accomplish more with less time, and that is what we are all aiming for.

Chapter 4 – Dissecting Procrastination and How Having a Protocol can Help you Avoid It

If procrastinators have been right all along, then tomorrow will be the busiest and the most hectic day of a person's life. Many people tend to delay the accomplishment of tasks for tomorrow, and that can be a very unhealthy attitude because it can have ill effects on your productivity. Many people fall into the trap of procrastination because it is a convenient thought and gives a false sense that tomorrow is a better day in terms of productivity.

"Stop when you are done. Do not stop when you are tired. Rest if you must, but do not stop until you finish the designated task." This quotation can help you get that internal motivation to deal with procrastination and find a solution to this problem. Remember, tomorrow is never promised, so you have to do what you can today. Things can be a bit complicated after you wake up the next day. Tasks tend to build up, and the situation might be more challenging to deal with later on.

Remember, procrastination should not be equated to resting for a while. Procrastination kills productivity, so you need to avoid falling into this trap by all means. Procrastination, take note, is taking deliberate and conscious efforts to delay or put aside duties and tasks that should have been done now. In this chapter, we set a protocol to help you avoid procrastination.

Procrastination Stopper Protocol #1: Promise yourself you will finish what you started.

Whenever you think of taking that first step, imagine the glory you will feel once you take the last step. Beginning a journey is indeed difficult and challenging in itself, but carrying on until you finish is another. If you know the meaning of the word "regret," and if you have experienced it yourself and did not like it, then make a pledge of finishing what you have started. Once you begin anything, promise to finish it. Do not think about quitting because it deprives you of those good night sleeps. Unfinished businesses are usually the trigger of the nastiest nightmares.

Procrastination Stopper Protocol #2: Be decisive and apply what you learned in the chapter on being decisive.

Every once in a while, a person might find himself in a situation where he is fast approaching a certain crossroad or decision point. Make a move swiftly and decide which turn you want to take. Do not fall into the trap of paralysis by analysis. Take a stand and decide right away before you lose any significant opportunities. Indecisiveness might lead to a situation you regret, and yes, productivity might suffer in the long run.

Procrastination Stopper Protocol #3: Psyche yourself and give yourself an extra push.

Always reassure yourself that there is no such thing as an impossible task. The tasks ahead of you are all manageable if you try. Nothing is difficult, if you only have the sheer will. Remember, discouraging yourself does not help at all. Everyone is equipped with the skill and the talent to get through any task.

What some people lack is the motivation and the determination. The most important push comes from within, and it comes from you.

Procrastination Stopper Protocol #4: Arrange the tasks in such a way that the downhill pattern is followed.

Begin with the most difficult tasks first. Follow the analogy of climbing a mountain. Of course, you have to go up first before you can enjoy the privilege of going downhill. You have to take on the difficult and the more challenging tasks first, and everything else will follow. In terms of productivity, you need to ride on constant momentum and this is the key to achieving more.

Procrastination Stopper Protocol #5: By all means, make a move.

Not making a move can be equated to giving in to procrastination. If you are too comfortable in not doing anything, chances are, you will maintain that state for quite a while. Most likely, it will be followed by episodes and hours of daydreaming. In order to avoid this, keep yourself busy and do something. Do anything significant to bring you closer to your goal. How can you reach the finish line if you do not take the initiative to take a single step?

Procrastination Stopper Protocol #6: Speaking of taking the first step, try taking that first step, no matter how small it may be.

You do not have to pole vault for a start. Of course, you have to take on the momentum and begin with a comfortable first baby step. You may take a small step, but make sure it is a step forward. It is not about having significant progress at first, it is about feeling the urge to do it and finish it. Once you can take the first step, you may find that the rest follows with ease. This gives you the urge to push yourself until you reach the finish line, and it is worth noting that old Chinese proverb that says all journeys start with one step.

Procrastination Stopper Protocol #7: Do not every give in to your fears.

Dwelling on your fear is pointless because it only leads to failure. On the other hand, taking courage to face your fear leads to success. Be courageous enough, and it will take you somewhere. Of course, you have to constantly evaluate whether you need to build up on your strengths and downplay your weaknesses. Face what you fear, and you might find that it was pointless to dwell on your fear in the first place. Most importantly, try to step out of your comfort zone to help you broaden your horizons.

Chapter 5 – Path toward Productivity: Be 100 Percent Procrastination-Free!

Much has been said about productivity, and we have only barely defined procrastination. In the previous chapter, we have suggested ways to "kill" procrastination, but we need to learn how to maintain the state of being procrastination-free. This is challenging because we often find ourselves falling into the trap of procrastination.

If you think of life as a big game, the procrastination is the "pause" button. It does not give you an edge over the game or over your opponents; it merely defers or delays your progress. In the end, you have to resume the game and face your fate. Procrastination is just a tactic to prolong your agony. Imagine, if only you were brave enough to face your fate right away, there are only two things to expect: (1) success, which you can savor right away, and (2) failure, from which you can learn important lessons. Delaying it, likewise, leads to two things: (1) an expired success, which you can no longer call a "legitimate" kind of success, and (2) a bigger kind of failure, which you cannot undo or remedy.

At this point, you need to say "yes" to become procrastination-free because it should be part of your protocol. You have to be free from procrastination for the rest of your life – but the question is: "How?" In this chapter, you learn how to do this while realizing your dreams and goals, gaining significant progress in your plan, and achieving professional and personal growth.

By saying no to procrastination, you will soon realize that you have a mission in life. Your worth is greater than you originally thought. You will learn to value your time more. Additionally, you can see there is a more efficient way to complete your work, and in effect, no amount of effort should be wasted.

Reason NOT to Procrastinate #1: Other people depend on you.

Perhaps you have not realized it yet, but you can truly create a lasting kind of impact on the lives of the people around you. You are more than just a social being – you are actually a blessing – that is, if you refrain from procrastinating. Extend a helping hand by being generous enough to share your inherent gifts and talents. If you do not procrastinate, you can contribute significantly to the success of the people around you. That way, even without knowing it, you are actually empowering and enriching the lives of other people.

Reason NOT to Procrastinate #2: You are a significant being.

You can create something truly significant, if you do not delay your progress. There is no way of knowing how far you can go unless you begin your life journey today. The borders are not set and the horizon is just an illusion. Choose to be free from procrastination. That way, you might find the possibilities truly thrilling and exhilarating. Being the best you can be is a possibility if you do not procrastinate. If you create high quality habits and adopt the protocols suggested in this book, your potential is boundless. There is no such thing as "impossible." There might be difficult and challenging tasks ahead, but you know you can manage them.

Reason NOT to Procrastinate #3: The possibility of being assigned to bigger and more fulfilling tasks.

Every single good thing and every single opportunity begins with small victories and successes. Your past tasks may be small, but the way you handled them is a good indicator of what you can possibly do in the future. In the end, if you veer away from procrastination, you can see you are moving on to bigger things. As you conquer each, your victories also become bigger, and in the end, it becomes more and more fulfilling. This means that the people around you are starting to believe you are worthy of their trust and that you are properly equipped. In short, they see you as somebody who has what it takes to gain bigger victories.

Reason NOT to Procrastinate #4: Tomorrow is never promised.

Since every single second, minute, hour, or day might be the last, one has to make sure that he is maximizing the time given to him. He has to make the most out of it. Do not procrastinate because 24-hour periods can be meaningless if you choose to not act at all. Wasting your time might seem convenient, but in the long run, you will realize that you cannot take back all the time you lost.

Reason NOT to Procrastinate #5: You are capable; you just have to be confident.

There is no point classifying tasks as "big" or "small." There are two kinds of tasks: those that you have successfully accomplished and those you failed to accomplish. Be procrastination-free and you can find yourself finishing one task after another. You then can enjoy two things: (1) the process, and (2) the results.

According to research, procrastination is actually very widespread. It is actually an underestimated epidemic. On a regular basis, 80 to 90 percent of the people around us are actually very consistently procrastinating. Every single minute, someone you know fails at battling procrastination. Now, more than ever, with the rise of technology, procrastination has become very powerful.

However, you are stronger than procrastination. You are better than procrastination. You can beat procrastination if you truly want to.

Chapter 6 – How to Maximize Productivity During the First Hours of your Day

The first hours of the day are statistically proven to be the most productive. You get more done during these hours because you are not yet distracted, and you are still in the zone. This finding is true across different jobs and careers. If you wish to become truly productive, you might want to consider starting early and utilizing the first few hours of the day for making significant progress.

By utilizing the first few hours wisely, you get to: (1) start your day on the right note, (2) be inclined to do more, (3) gain the necessary momentum, and (4) feel good about yourself. These are just some of the benefits, but ultimately, it boils down to the maximization of your productivity.

The suggested protocol items in this chapter will help you maximize those early hours. At the end of the day, you can proudly say you achieved a lot.

Early Hours Maximization Tip #1: Work your mood out.

Of course, you need to be physically, emotionally, and psychologically ready – these three aspects greatly affect a person's mood. Nobody else can do anything about stabilizing your mood except yourself. Keep in touch with what you feel and try, by all means, to feel good about yourself. This way, you are ready to take on any challenge, especially during the first few hours of the day. Analyzing your mood also helps you get to know yourself better. From the reflection, you know how to improve.

Early Hours Maximization Tip #2: Reply to emails that are deemed urgent; do the same for phone calls.

If the emails are not urgent and if the phone calls are not important, then they can wait. Go back to them later in the day. This way, you can minimize your distractions.

Early Hours Maximization Tip #3: Spend the first 15 minutes lining up your tasks and organizing your workspace.

If you can afford it, work on a clear desk. If you can put stuff in the drawers, do so. Put away all the things you do not need. This sets the mood right because there is less of a chance of becoming distracted. Set that tone as early as possible, and you can only do this if you clear or at least arrange your desk early in the morning. This not only cuts down the possibility of confusion, it also saves time.

Early Hours Maximization Tip #4: Do not deprive yourself of breaks.

Since you started early, you deserve to take a break. Yes, you are encouraged to be productive as early as possible, but you are warned not to get too exhausted or burned out too early. Remember, you deserve to take a 10 to 15 minute break to renew your drive. This is essential for maintaining your momentum.

Early Hours Maximization Tip #5: Take full advantage of your mind that is still in the clearest and the most refreshed state.

The brain works at its optimum at the beginning of the day. The creative juices seem to overflow during this period, and of course, you want to use that. You do not literally want to see those creative juices, along with other bright ideas, go down the drain.

Early Hours Maximization Tip #6: Be present during the first few hours in the morning.

Most of the tasks are already half done if you simply show up. Physical presence is quite an assurance that you complete the goal. Readiness of the physical, emotional, and mental aspects is essential for you to be able to complete the task.

Early Hours Maximization Tip #7: Constantly remind yourself that you want to be productive.

Remind yourself of your purpose because this assists you in taking the correct direction. The purpose needs to be clear to you, and you must remind yourself of that purpose. You have to tell yourself constantly, so you are properly motivated. If you have the inner drive, your productivity will be strong for the rest of the day – not just during the early hours.

Early Hours Maximization Tip #8: Chat with your co-workers and colleagues.

You have to be careful not to spend too much time doing this, but it can be good for your mental state. Also, you have to align your chatting session with your productivity goals and objectives. Let everyone know what you desire to achieve that day. By publicizing your plan to others and encouraging them to do the same, your individual drive can have a positive effect on everyone. Keep track of the team goals. Commit not just to yourself, but to others as well. Most importantly, try to establish the connections and links needed so you can work with ease and confidence in your workplace.

Early Hours Maximization Tip #9: Always begin on a clean slate.

This is the privilege that is continuously offered to us each morning we wake up to. Forget about the shortcomings and the mistakes you made yesterday. Today is new day, another start. If ever you feel like you underperformed a bit in the previous day, you can always compensate for it today.

Maximizing the early hours will surely get you on track. It also helps you to develop healthy habits, and these can positively influence your productivity level. Research shows that the first hours of the morning are the best time to set the right mood. Have you ever heard of starting off on the right foot? This is one of the best analogies to taking advantage of your mornings. By being productive in the morning, you get to feel good about yourself and your job. This only gives you more focus and optimism.

Chapter 7 – Killing Procrastination is a Mental Game

Once adulthood is reached, the human brain has also reached a point where the brain has a variety of pathways to take in new information very efficiently. Because of these established pathways, the processing of information becomes very fast. These pathways will be of help when problems come up and solutions are needed. With time, these pathways lead to instant solutions because of the factor of familiarity. When you become familiar with frequent problems, it becomes easier for you to focus and concentrate. In the end, this factor has a great effect on productivity.

Productivity is a game of the brain. By focusing on strengthening your brain, you can enhance your productivity, but how can you strengthen your brain? Of course, you have to continuously perform brain exercises to hone your mental capabilities. Pushing your brain to function helps you better combat procrastination, thereby giving you better chances of improving your productivity. You can also give all the focus and concentration due for each of the tasks at hand.

To give an example, many exercises that require manipulation by the hands make good brain exercises because these can directly stimulate brain activity. Some examples are sketching, juggling balls, making mosaics, getting involved in pottery making, doing simple needlework, strumming the guitar, playing the piano, and even playing table tennis. Actually, it is better if you involve more senses because it gives your brain more sources of stimulation and leads to better levels of temporal and critical reasoning, spatial capabilities, and creativity.

Perhaps, at this point, you are already lured to getting involved in mental calisthenics and exercises for the brain. However, take note that before doing so you need to choose very carefully. To guide you in the selection process, you might consider following these criteria:

Brain Exercise Standard #1: The activity you choose should be challenging for you.

Truth be told, any activity can qualify under this standard, but it actually depends on you. What do you find too easy? What is too challenging? Therefore, you have to ask yourself, "Do I really find this activity challenging?" Assess how much mental or intellectual effort you are exerting for a certain task. There are many examples from which you can choose. These are highly recommended by experts: gaining mastery of a new language in terms of speaking and writing, learning how to play a new instrument, familiarizing oneself and actually playing a different kind of sport, and trying to solve different mathematical or analytical types of problems.

Brain Exercise Standard #2: Try something new and unfamiliar to you.

To truly challenge your mind, you have to choose an activity you have not encountered before. If you choose something you have done already or you are already familiar with, there is a great chance that you will only need minimal effort to figure it out. If it is not challenging, then it is not a good brain exercise. Finally, a good brain enhancing exercise pushes you and encourages you to move out of your usual zone of comfort.

Brain Exercise Standard #3: Try out something enjoyable and fun.

Physical, emotional, and even intellectual types of fun are also important. These help you make more brain improvement. Fun helps you become more committed and sincerely interested. If you wish to get the most out of the effort you are exerting, then you should have fun at the very least. Yes, one factor is that it should be very challenging, but it should not be frustrating. It should be fun and appealing to as many senses as possible.

Chapter 8 – Productivity and Laughter

Yes, you read it right. There is a chapter devoted for laughter, but what is laughter exactly?

Laughter is one of the many natural reactions of human beings used to express happiness and contentment. It involves rhythmic contractions of the person's diaphragm. It has an audible manifestation, and it can be very contagious. When was the last time you laughed just because you heard someone else laughing? You might even find yourself chuckling along even if you do not know the reason for the laughter.

The next time you hear jokes in the middle of a busy day, do not feel guilty for stopping your work and indulging in a good laugh. After all, listening to funny lines and trying to come up with your own also helps in the process of activating several portions of your brain. This clearly helps in improving your concentration, capability to learn and your level of creativity – all of which are useful in your work, regardless of your profession.

These are some of the tips you might consider following to enhance levels of productivity in the workplace with the aid of laughter.

Seriously Funny Tip #1: Have some regular fun, but be careful not to indulge in it too much.

Having fun is not a crime. It is encouraged for you to have fun with other people, and you can socialize with them, too, in the process. Be a person who readily smiles or laughs. That makes you easy to get along with. Getting along with others is essential in creating a team spirit. Therefore, a good laugh and having fun can actually be more productive than you think. Just keep in mind how much fun you are having because you do have tasks to accomplish. Always be reminded of that.

Seriously Funny Tip #2: Laugh at your own mistakes and take your silliness lightly.

It is okay to be embarrassed and talk about it from time to time. After all, nobody is truly perfect. Take your job and duties seriously, but you have to be easy on yourself at times. Instead of dwelling on your past imperfections, move on and move forward. The best way to move on is to take it easy and not be too serious when it comes to your mistakes. Have fun in the middle of your mistakes, and you will see how your productivity improves in the long run. To emphasize, you do not have to be perfect in order to be productive.

Seriously Funny Tip #3: Do not deprive yourself of a good laugh.

If you feel you need to let out a loud laugh, let loose. The worst feeling is not being able to laugh when you feel you need to. If you are a bit stressed, look for people laughing. Listen to their laughter or join in their conversation and in their laughter; your mood will instantly improve. Do not ever be afraid to laugh because there are a lot of reasons to do so.

This is how an old adage put it: "The best medicine is laughter." However, did you know that laughter can also help you become a more productive individual? In the simplest terms, it has something to do with elevating the level of focus and concentration. Yes, laughter greatly helps in improving these two aspects.

Chapter 9 – Some Suggested Protocols on Setting Meaningful Goals for Better Productivity

On a more serious note, productivity is an impossible task to tackle if you do not know how to create meaningful goals. Goals give your life direction, and you have to take the task of setting goals quite seriously. Hopefully, upon reading this chapter, you will have a better idea on what goals you should set and how to set them.

Take note that human beings are capable of moving up one notch in terms of performance, and they are more efficient when they are aware of their goals. Being aware of one's goals requires well defined and clearly expressed aims, so one has to be aware on how to properly set goals to improve productivity.

Every single time you set your goals, you need to clearly assess and evaluate each of them, so you can find sufficient reason to commit to each of them. First, you must have a very clear vision of what results you want. Second, you have to be sincere in believing that your goals are attainable, even if they are challenging. Third, you have to truly commit not just to yourself, but also to others. Being accountable always improves productivity.

These are some points of consideration whenever you find yourself with the daunting task of setting significant and meaningful goals for yourself or for your organization:

Point of Consideration #1: Look into the process by which you create your goals and constantly assess its effectiveness.

If you are working alone, you have to be completely aware of the reasons why you create your goals. This helps you own your goals. On the other hand, if you work in a group or an organization, try to get as many individuals as possible involved in the goal-making process. When there is a sense of ownership, there is a greater chance that you will see the goal through to completion. As much as possible, never force a goal on anyone because that can be very intimidating and there will be no sense of ownership.

Point of Consideration #2: Consider the level of difficulty and complexity of the task that is aligned with the goal that has to be set.

Even before setting any goals, you need to thoroughly evaluate yourself and your capabilities. Are you truly capable of taking on the challenge? Can you truly meet the demands the task might involve? If you find it too complicated, do not proceed yet. Instead, equip yourself so that next time, you feel more capable.

Point of Consideration #3: Look into how near or how far you are from success and how easy or difficult each goal is.

According to the Theory of the Temporal Type of Motivation, goal setting should consider precursors like level of difficulty of the goal and the proximity of success during the process identifying your aims. Therefore, you need to consider if the goal will be worth it even before you set it.

Point of Consideration #4: Establish a mechanism for clear feedback.

As much as possible, have someone monitor your level of achievement and progress. This has to be constantly checked, so you know if you are able to attain your goals based on the expected rate you initially set. The feedback mechanism lets you know what you are doing right and if there are things you can improve or eliminate. In addition, evaluation would be a lot easier if you have a clear mechanism for feedback. At the end of the day, even in the aspect of setting goals, it is important to know if you are doing things right.

With these important considerations, you can create important goals that are truly significant and meaningful. Meaningful goals lead to more meaningful achievements. Meaningful achievements give more dimensions to success. In addition, successes are easier to value if you find deeper significance in your achievements.

Chapter 10 – Transforming Habits into Protocols

When protocols are absorbed and applied in everyday living, they become habits. Habits have a deeper level of significance, and they bear greater meaning in life.

Aristotle once pointed out that we are what we continuously and consistently do. That defines our character, our passion, and our direction. Aristotle further said that excellence is not merely a single act that is outstanding, but it is a series of consistent acts. Therefore, in the end, Aristotle concluded that excellence is not just a mere act – excellence is a habit. In order to truly be a winner in the battle of life, one has to create protocols that will soon become habits that ultimately lead to success.

Without a doubt, creating new habits can be very challenging. It can be the most difficult task that you may encounter. It is difficult, in a sense, because in the first place, no one has a ready answer for the question, "How can you create a habit and stick to it?"

Experts divulge their new discovery regarding habit creation and its relationship with personal rituals. These are further analyzed to see their effects to the overall quality of the lives of people. The results show that it is a person's personal habits and rituals that help him attain success. When you get used to your habits, they are transformed into rituals, thereby deeply embedding them in your system. In the long run, the rituals become protocols, and that is what this book is all about.

As you can see, the construction of this book has always been in the form of suggestion – that is because it is really impossible to *impose* protocols. They are somewhat learned and acquired over a period of time. Even companies and industries have to prove that practices are time-tested and appropriate for their needs before they are formally adopted as protocols. That is how it works.

Now, you see how important it is to come up with habits that are high quality. Once you decide to form high quality habits, you will feel the instantaneous effect. High quality protocols emanate from high quality rituals, which in turn originate from high quality habits. These high quality habits are formed with the aim of cutting down the level of exposure to distractions, which are the biggest obstacles to increased productivity.

Habit Formation Step #1: Have the inner determination and will to give you natural motivation.

Your courage and strength should be drawn from your inner determination and will. Whenever you feel like giving up on a certain habit, try to draw strength from your inner motivation. This gives you more reason to stick to your high quality habit. Remind yourself of your goals every day. You will see that habit formation becomes more manageable.

Habit Formation Step #2: Understand the natural inclination of human beings to create habits.

After all, people are habit-driven creatures, and as a person who aspires to create habits, you have to understand this fact. However, if you deal with habit formation in a more scientific sense, you will see that habits can only be successfully acquired if you use a definite pattern, with the same state of mind, with similar thoughts, and with the same course of action over a certain amount of time. There are psychologists who say that if you can stick to a certain action for 21 days straight days, then it becomes a habit.

Habit Formation Step #3: Learn one habit at a time.

Just like the tasks, you do not have to master more than one habit at a time. It is always better if to focus on one now and learn another at a different time. It should be recognized that learning a habit is not a joke, and it cannot be rushed. If you want to learn and put to test habits like taking on a healthy lifestyle, rising early, or quitting smoking, then you have to give each of these habits enough time to sink in. The designation of a time window will help you become more triumphant with each of the habits you wish to take on.

Habit Formation Step #4: Start the habit and stick to it.

You do not need to devote a lot of time for preparation. Actually, experts say the sooner you start the habit, the better, and once you start it, never think about deviating. You have to be unswerving, dedicated, persevering, and persistent.

Additionally, waiting for the perfect time to start might lead you to forget why you wanted to start in the first place. If you let a day, a week, or a month to pass before saying you are "ready," you might end up not starting at all. Therefore, instead of waiting, why not start right at this very moment. The difficulty will dramatically decrease once you begin.

Starting a habit is one thing, but sticking to the habit is another. Have faith in the habit and have faith in yourself. Several adjustments have to be made, indeed, and it will not be easy at all. You have to make some changes in your environment, and it might not be easy. Whatever changes you have to make, make them quick.

Meaningful habits can be created using the steps above. With time, they become rituals in a very natural manner. Just do it unceasingly and you will find it unstoppable. However, how can you transform such habits and rituals into protocols? Here is how:

Transforming Habits to Protocol Step #1: Explore the window of maximum productivity.

The period of time within the day where you are on your toes in terms of productivity is often called the "productive window." If you are aware of that period of high productivity, then you can try doing your habits during this period of time. Habits done during the productive window are very likely to be absorbed as your personal protocol.

Transforming Habits to Protocol Step #2: Have the aim to at least complete.

Never fall into the trap of getting lured by the notion of perfection. Perfection is reserved for the gods, and you are not a god. Perfection does its job well in setting expectations and standards, but as a human being, try to be more realistic. Raise the bar high enough, but not too high to the point that you cannot reach.

Transforming Habits to Protocol Step #3: Assess the surroundings, and make the necessary adjustments.

Of course, it is not possible for you to do it all alone. You need some help. If there are no other people to help you out, then you have to find all the help you need from your environment. For example, if you wish to begin a habit of waking up at 4:30 AM, then you might need to set an alarm. Likewise, you need to assure that your sleep is distraction-free, so you can get the maximum amount of rest despite rising early. In the same manner, if you wish to make a habit of not browsing through Facebook on your smart phone, then you might need to uninstall the app. You must create an environment conducive to progress and productivity. This is essential for attaining success.

Transforming Habits to Protocol Step #4: Begin with the more challenging habits first.

The habits that are the most challenging to live by should be transformed into protocols first. By beginning with the most challenging first, everything else will be easy to tackle. If you have been through the worst first, everything else is bound to get better.

Now, you are fully equipped with the knowledge needed to transform habits to protocols. If you have protocols, becoming more productive is easier, even if tasks get more daunting and more challenging. With these four steps, you can acquire the skills you need to become a more responsible and productive individual.

Conclusion

I hope this book was able to help you become more productive and avoid procrastination.

The next step is to apply what you have learned in this book. There are many situations in everyday life and in the workplace that can be improved by the suggestions in this book.

Thank you and good luck!

www.ingramcontent.com/pod-product-compliance
Lightning Source LLC
Chambersburg PA
CBHW070508290526
45790CB00003B/1141

* 9 7 8 1 5 0 3 2 0 6 7 6 2 *